Summary of

The Silent Wife

A. S. A. Harrison

Conversation Starters

By BookHabits

Tips for Using BookHabits Conversation Starters:

EVERY GOOD BOOK CONTAINS A WORLD FAR DEEPER THAN the surface of its pages. The characters and their world come alive through the words on the pages, yet the characters and its world still live on. Questions herein are designed to bring us beneath the surface of the page and invite us into the world that lives on. These questions can be used to:

- Foster a deeper understanding of the book
- Promote an atmosphere of discussion for groups
- Assist in the study of the book, either individually or corporately
- Explore unseen realms of the book as never seen before

About Us:

THROUGH YEARS OF EXPERIENCE AND FIELD EXPERTISE, from newspaper featured book clubs to local library chapters, *BookHabits* can bring your book discussion to life. Host your book party as we discuss some of today's most widely read books.

Table of Contents

Introducing *The Silent Wife*.. 6

Discussion Questions 10

Introducing the Author 31

Fireside Questions... 35

Quiz Questions 54

Quiz Answers... 67

Ways to Continue Your Reading 68

Introducing *The Silent Wife*

JODI BRETT AND TODD GILBERT LIVED THE PERFECT, charmed life of a power couple in Chicago, or so it seemed. Together for twenty years, their lives were a carefully planned routine of work and travel. Jodi has everything that she ever wanted, and that's okay for her, until everything crumbles and their apparently faultless relationship begins to collapse right before their very eyes. Now Jodi will be forced to face the long-time deception that she has tried her best to ignore in hopes that it will go away as Todd makes a decision that will finally change both their lives as they know it.

A.S.A. Harrison's first and only psychological thriller talks about cheating and the effects it has on people. Told from a "his" and "her" perspective reminiscent of Gillian Flynn's *New York Times* hit, *Gone Girl,* the novel appeals to the reader as it gives one an omniscient idea of what is happening between the two main characters and how different things are from their perspective. Though both Jodi and Todd seem likable in the beginning, Harrison's use of colorful language gives an image of a marriage under false pretenses that is nearing its dissolution that should have happened a long time ago. Every word and sentence written by Harrison is a meticulous preparation for the final act that will change their lives forever, which has been promised since the first chapter. Though already revealed what Jodi will become, the author's masterful weaving of scenes and flashbacks seem to convince the reader somehow that it might not happen at all and by some ingenious twist, things will be different than they seem.

While Harrison ultimately did not see the fruit of her labor in print, she received an advanced review copy. *The Silent Wife* opened to critical acclaim and immediately hit No.2 on the *New York Times* Best Seller list. The author passed away in April 2013 from cancer, only weeks before the novel was published. At the time of her demise, she was already working on her second novel. A.S.A.

Harrison is also the author of four non-fiction stories.

Discussion Questions

"Get Ready to Enter a New World"

Tip: Begin with questions dealing with broader issues to ensure ample time for quality discussions. Read through all discussion questions before engaging.

question 1

Jodi still sees herself as a young woman. How do you think it affected the way she reacted to Todd's unfaithfulness to her?

~~~

~~~

question 2

Jodi likes to "throw herself" into everything she does. How do you think her passion affected the way she contemplated getting back at Todd?

~~~

~~~

question 3

Jodi met Todd in a car accident when she was distracted, and he gave her an earful of tirade. Do you think it was a proper response given the circumstance? Do you think there is something else Todd could have done differently at that time? Explain.

~~~

question 4

Todd put his best foot forward during their first date. What difference would it have made to Jodi if he turned out to be just like the guys she used to go out with?

~~~

question 5

Todd is a serial womanizer. What difference do you think it would have made to Jodi if he had broken it off with the woman he was seeing on the side?

~~~

~~~

question 6

Jodi didn't want to have children like Todd did. Do you think it would have prompted Todd to change his cheating ways if Jodi considered having kids of her own? Why or why not?

~~~

~~~

question 7

Jodi likes to deny that something is wrong in her life. Do you think that if she had confronted Todd about his cheating ways from the beginning, she would not have resorted to murder in the end? Why or why not?

~~~

question 8

A.S.A. Harrison already revealed that Jodi would kill Todd from the beginning. Do you think it would have made the story better if the author had withheld that information first? Why or why not?

~~~

question 9

Jodi Brett and Todd Gilbert are not married. How do you think things would have ended differently for Todd if he had offered to marry Jodi?

~~~

~~~

question 10

The book was told in alternating voices of Jodi and Todd. Do you think this approach helped the reader to get a good grasp of both characters' minds at that given moment? Why or why not?

~~~

~~~

question 11

Natasha Kovacs, Todd's other woman, became pregnant with his child. Do you think it was right for him to offer marriage when he has been with Jodi longer? Why or why not?

~~~

question 12

At one point, Todd realized he liked his life with Jodi more than with Natasha. Do you think he might have made a mistake in rushing his life with Natasha and leaving Jodi alone after all their years together? Explain.

~~~

~~~

question 13

When Dean found out about Todd and his daughter Natasha's relationship, he got mad at his best friend. Do you think he reacted properly about the whole situation? How did it affect his relationship with Natasha?

~~~

~~~

question 14

The book was set in Illinois. How do you think Jodi's decision would have been different if they were residing in another city/state?

~~~

question 15

Todd's lawyer made it clear to Jodi that their status would not make her eligible to receive support in any way. Do you think that if Todd offered money and support to Jodi, she might have left him peacefully and moved on? Why or why not?

~~~

~~~

question 16

Many critics likened *The Silent Wife* to Gillian Flynn's *Gone Girl*. Do you think it would have reached the *NY Times* Best Seller list if it was not preceded by the success of Flynn's novel? Why or why not?

~~~

~ ~ ~

question 17

The book was told in an alternating "his" and "her" voice. Do you think this helped build the book as a successful psychological thriller? Why or why not?

~ ~ ~

~~~

question 18

The Huffington Post dubbed the novel as better than *Gone Girl*. Do you think that this comparison is justified? Explain.

~~~

~~~

question 19

The *Express UK* said the novel was impossible to put down because of its "rich language." How do you think that the author's use of language made the story more likable and realistic?

~~~

~~~

question 20

The Guardian said that Todd was "less fleshed out" in the novel. Do you think that this is true or that the understanding of his character is subjective?

~~~

Introducing the Author

A.S.A. HARRISON IS A CANADIAN WRITER WHOSE REAL name is Susan Harrison. Born in 1948 to a chemical engineer father and homemaker mother who dabbled in photography, it is no wonder that her inclination towards the arts has always been present in her life. Supported by her parents, she went to study at the Ontario College of Art, where her love for the vibrant artistic life and flair for drama and performing flourished.

It wasn't long before Harrison quit school and decided she wanted to write. While it remained unclear to her what genre she would focus on, she began doing research on topics and interests that seemed taboo and outrageous during that time. She began to talk to different women, which would become the basis of her first book, *Orgasms*, which was about sexual fulfillment in climax and the women who experience it. At this time, she had already married Rodney Werden, a video artist.

Harrison loved to do actual research for her works and at one time collaborated with striptease and performance artist Margaret Dragu for her second book, *Revelations: Essays on Striptease and Sexuality.*

Long after her divorce from her first husband, she met visual artist John Massey. This was at the same time she became intrigued with yoga and vegetarianism. Harrison eventually started work as an editor for a quarterly publication, *C Magazine,* which would later pave the way for her to write a feline astrology book, titled, *Zodicat Speaks.*

Eventually, her desire to expand the genre she's in prompted her to write mystery novels, which were not picked up and rejected by agents. But that did not stop Harrison from pursuing her passion. As she neared her mid-50s, she got the idea for a psychological thriller that would catapult her to the *NY Times* Best Seller list posthumously.

The final pages of *The Silent Wife* were written during her final bout with cancer, but that did not stop her from finishing it. Before succumbing to the illness, her work was picked up and was on its way to publication. Sadly, the disease took her in April, and she did not live to see it released in June of that year.

The novel is now picked up for a movie adaptation.

Fireside Questions

"What would you do?"

Tip: These questions can be a fun exercise as it spurs creativity among the readers by allowing alternate scene endings and "if this was you" questions.

~~~

question 21

The book's success was based on how the planning of the revenge was described as very "plausible." How do you think the realistic plot affected the reader's reception of the novel?

~~~

~~~

question 22

Sarah Weinman from *The New Republic* lauded the author's alternate style of writing. Do you think that the way the story was written helped build the characters more as it revealed each of their flaws slowly? Explain.

~~~

~~~

question 23

Because of its success, the novel is in the works to be adapted to the big screen. How do you think the film will be different from the actual book?

~~~

~ ~ ~

question 24

The novel was only published in a paperback format. Do you think that the format played a huge role in the success of the book and why?

~ ~ ~

~~~

question 25

The National Post said that one flaw of the novel is the "omniscient POV" employed by the author. Do you think that this is true for the story? Why or why not?

~~~

~~~

question 26

A.S.A. Harrison died from cancer before the novel was published. How do you think her demise influenced the reader's curiosity and reception for the book?

~~~

question 27

The author noted that some "concessions were not made" in the synopsis of the book. Do you think that compromise is very important in any marriage/relationship?

~~~

question 28

A.S.A. Harrison's real name is Susan Harrison. How do you think that living during the 1960s affected her decision to write under a pen name?

~~~

~~~

question 29

The author worked as a typesetter for the *Toronto Sun* and Gandalph Graphics before writing her first and only novel. Do you think her work environment gave her inspiration for *The Silent Wife* and how?

~~~

~~~

question 30

The way the characters treated one another in the novel paved the way for the ultimate revenge. Do you think that getting even is always the best solution for pain and hurt caused by someone? Why or why not?

~~~

question 31

Jodi Brett is a psychotherapist. How do you think things would have ended differently between her and her husband if her occupation were different?

~~~

question 32

There was no common-law marriage regulation in Illinois. How do you think Jodi would have reacted to Todd's indiscretion with Natasha if there were one in place?

~~~

~ ~ ~

question 33

If Jodi had gotten pregnant, do you think Todd would have chosen to be with her rather than Natasha? Why or why not?

~ ~ ~

~~~

question 34

If Todd had not offered to marry Natasha after he got her pregnant, what do you think would have been Jodi's reaction?

~~~

question 35

Natasha is Dean's daughter, Todd's best friend. If she weren't, do you think Dean would have approved of their relationship? Why or why not?

~~~

question 36

If Jodi had been open to the idea of having her own kids, what do you think would have happened to Todd's serial womanizing?

~~~

~ ~ ~

question 37

If the author had not worked as a typesetter, do you think she would have written the novel? Why or why not?

~ ~ ~

~~~

question 38

What do you think the reception of *The Silent Wife* would have been if it had not been compared to Gillian Flynn's *Gone Girl*?

~~~

Quiz Questions

"Ready to Announce the Winners?"

Tip: Create a leaderboard and track scores to see who gets the most correct answers. Winners required. Prizes optional.

quiz question 1

Jodi Brett's occupation is _____.

~~~

quiz question 2

True or false: The common-law marriage rule exist in Illinois.

~~~

quiz question 3

True or false: Jodi suffering from a mental health problem when she committed the crime.

quiz question 4

True or false: Todd offered to marry Natasha after he found out she was pregnant.

~ ~ ~

quiz question 5

True or false: Todd's lawyers offered monetary support to Jodi after he told her to vacate their Chicago house.

quiz question 6

True or false: There were multiple suspects in the murder of Todd?

~ ~ ~

quiz question 7

True or false: Dean was delighted to know his daughter was pregnant with his grandchild.

~ ~ ~

~~~

quiz question 8

A.S.A. Harrison died from _____.

~~~

quiz question 9

True or false: The author was writing a sequel to the story when she passed away.

~~~

quiz question 10

True or false: Harrison wrote six nonfiction books in addition to *The Silent Wife*.

~~~

~~~

quiz question 11

A.S.A. Harrison was a _____ before she began writing books.

~~~

~~~

quiz question 12

The author was married _____.

~~~

Quiz Answers

1. psychotherapist
2. false; there is no common law marriage rule
3. false; Judi did not suffer from a mental disability
4. true
5. false; they did not offer monetary support
6. True
7. false; it was not good news to him
8. cancer
9. false; she did not write any other books
10. false; she only wrote one book
11. typesetter
12. twice

Ways to Continue Your Reading

EVERY month, our team runs through a wide selection of books to pick the best titles for readers and reading groups, and promotes these titles to our thousands of readers – sometimes with free downloads, sale dates, and additional brochures.

If you have not yet read the original work or would like to read it again, get the book here.

Want to register yourself or a book group? It's free and takes 1-click.

Register here.

On the Next Page...

Please write us your reviews! Any length would be fine but we'd appreciate hearing you more! We'd be SO grateful.

Till next time,

BookHabits

"Loving Books is Actually a Habit"